THE BEGINNING...

MY INTRODUCTION

Before I start....just a brief introduction about me!

____

____

____

____

____

____

____

____

____

Name:

Signature

Date

My Grandmother's
Journal

We love to receive reviews from our customers. If you had the opportunity to provide a review we would greatly appreciate it.

Thank you!

A Place to Share My Life Memories.

Grandmother xx

My Lifetime Legacy Journal

THE BEGINNING.....

Full Name at Birth

____

Date of Birth   /   /   _______________________

Time of Birth   :   ________________________

Day of the week you were born?
____

Height at birth? (if known)
____

Weight at birth? (If known)
____

Your Place of Birth (include the City/Town, Country)

____

Did you have any siblings when you were born? If so, what were their names and their ages?

____

____

____

ADD ANY ADDITIONAL NOTES OR INFORMATION HERE...

THE BEGINNING.....

Share with us some information about your parents?

____

____

____

____

Were you in good health as a baby?

____

____

____

Did you have any unique characteristics or funny things you did as a baby?

____

____

____

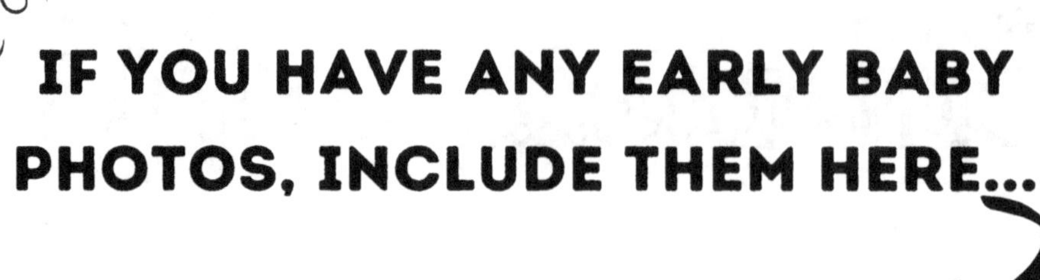

IF YOU HAVE ANY EARLY BABY PHOTOS, INCLUDE THEM HERE...

THE BEGINNING.....

Were you an active or quiet baby?

Were you ever told what your first words were?

Do you have any other baby memories to share?

"There is no influence so powerful as that of a mother."

—Sara Josepha Hale

FAMILY HISTORY

This is our Family Tree!

FAMILY HISTORY

My grandparents names were:

Grandmother (Fathers Side): ___________________

Grandfather (Fathers Side) ___________________

Grandmother (Mothers Side): ___________________

Grandfather (Mothers Side) ___________________

They were born in: (country)

Grandmother (Fathers Side): ___________________

Grandfather (Fathers Side) ___________________

Grandmother (Mothers Side): ___________________

Grandfather (Mothers Side) ___________________

This is something that not many people may know about our family history......

____

____

____

Additional Family History information:

____

____

____

Grandfather

Grandfather

Grandmother

Grandmother

Mother

Father

Me

ADD ANY ADDITIONAL NOTES OR INFORMATION HERE...

CHILDHOOD YEARS

CHILDHOOD YEARS....

What was your favorite toy growing up?

Did you have a pet or any pets growing up?

What was your favorite T.V show to watch as a child?

Was there a moment you remember getting into big trouble as a child? Was there a punishment?

ADD ANY ADDITIONAL NOTES OR INFORMATION HERE...

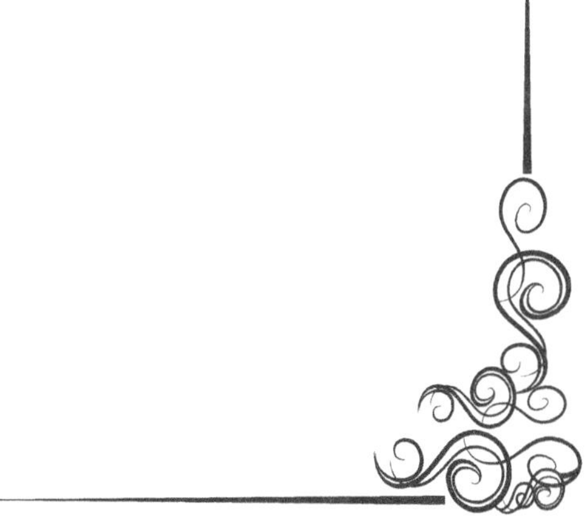

CHILDHOOD YEARS....

What are your fondest memories growing up between the ages of 5 - 12 years?

____

____

____

____

____

____

____

____

____

____

____

IF YOU HAVE ANY EARLY CHILDHOOD PHOTOS, PLACE THEM HERE...

CHILDHOOD YEARS....

What was your favorite meal as a child?

____

What elementary/primary school did you attend and where was it located?

____

____

Describe your most memorable moment or story from elementary/primary school.

____

____

____

____

____

____

____

CHILDHOOD YEARS....

Where did you grow up as a child?
(house, location, town etc)

____

____

____

____

Who was your best friend or your best friends as a child?

____

____

____

What was your favorite day of the week and why?

____

____

____

____

____

DO YOU HAVE ANY SCHOOL PHOTOS, OR OTHER DETAILS TO SHARE?

TEENAGE YEARS

TEENAGE YEARS....

Describe your dress sense and clothing as a teenager. Is there anything that stands out for you?

____

____

____

When and where did you learn to drive a vehicle?

____

____

What was your first vehicle and how much did you purchase it for? Tell us your special 'first car' story!

____

____

____

____

____

____

INCLUE ANY 'FIRST VEHICLE' PHOTOS OR OTHER INFORMATION HERE..

TEENAGE YEARS....

What High School did you attend and where was it located?

____

____

____

Who was you favorite teacher or coach and why?

____

____

____

What was your favorite subject at school?

____

____

____

Did you date anyone at High School?

____

____

____

SHARE ANY FURTHER DETAILS HERE

TEENAGE YEARS....

What hobbies did you have as a teenager?

What is your most memorable moment as a teenager?

If you knew what you know today, what would you have done differently as a teenager?

SHARE ANY OTHER DETAILS OR
MEMORIES HERE

TEENAGE YEARS....

Did you have a close friendship group? Have you maintained contact with any of them?

____

____

____

____

____

Did you have any nicknames at High School?

____

____

What 5 words come to mind to describe your teenage years?

1. ____

2. ____

3. ____

4. ____

5. ____

WHEN I WAS..

WHEN I WAS....

When I was a child, my mode of transport to school was..

____

____

When I was in my teens, the biggest news story that I recall was .....

____

____

____

When I was growing up, my 3 favorite movies were:

1. ______________________________________

2. ______________________________________

3. ______________________________________

WHEN I WAS....

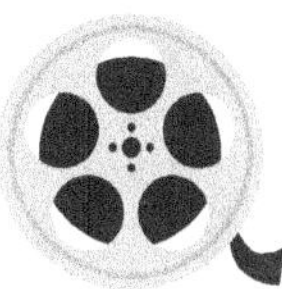

When I was a child, the first movie I went to the theatre to see was..

When I graduated from elementary/primary school, the year was..

When I was a child, I wanted to be a......

When I was 18 years old, my favorite music and band was..

When I was in my teens, the most popular thing to do on a Saturday night was.......

When I was young, I loved to travel to.......

SHARE ANY FURTHER TRAVEL MEMORIES HERE..

PARENTHOOD

PARENTHOOD....

How old were you when you first became a parent?

Explain how you felt emotionally when you became a parent for the first time?

Where were you located (city/town/country) when you had your first child?

SHARE SOME PARENTING PHOTOS HERE..

PARENTHOOD....

What has been the biggest challenge for you as a parent?

____

____

____

____

____

What are 3 key responsibilities you believe are important as a parent?

1 ____

____

2 ____

____

3 ____

____

PARENTHOOD....

When did you first become a grandparent? Share some
information about when you became a grandparent.

EXPAND ON ANY FURTHER PARENTING
MEMORIES YOU MAY LIKE TO SHARE

MORE ABOUT ME!

MORE ABOUT ME....

Not many people know this about me, so let me share it with you:

____

____

____

____

____

____

____

The activity or hobby that I enjoy most to do now is.....

____

____

I have the unique ability to be able to....

____

____

MORE ABOUT ME....

If I was able to go back to a special time in history, it would be...

____

____

____

If I could pass on one word of advice to others, it would be..

____

____

____

There are special moments in life that you wish you could pause to enjoy for longer. Mine would be......

____

____

____

____

____

MORE ABOUT ME....

I wish I had the opportunity to...

____

____

____

The quote that resonates most with me is..

____

____

____

____

My favorite book of all time is:

____

If there is one thing I would like to be remembered for it would be:

____

____

____

____

MORE ABOUT ME....

When I look back on my life so far, my 3 proudest moments are:

1

2

3

If there were 3 famous people that I could invite for dinner they would be:

1

2

3

MORE ABOUT ME....

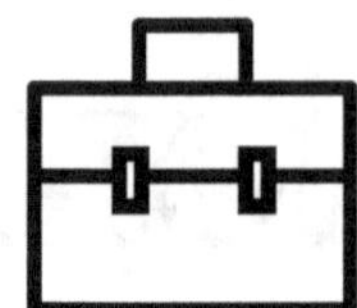

From my teen years, these are the jobs that I've had:

MORE ABOUT ME....

One of the jobs that stands out as my most enjoyable has been..

____

____

The most interesting place I have ever traveled to has been.... (include the year/date this occurred)

____

____

____

If I was given a free return flight to anywhere in the world, I would visit...(include your 'Why')

____

____

____

____

____

SOME EXTRA SPACE FOR INFORMATION OR PHOTOS HERE..

FINAL NOTES

FINAL NOTES....

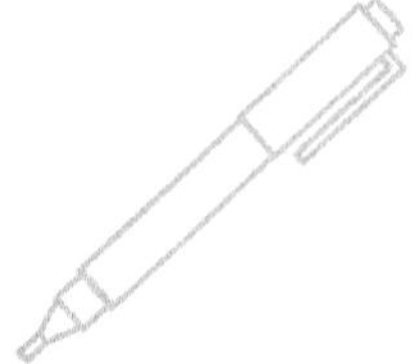

There have been many questions that I have answered in this book, but I would also like to share this with you...

your time to write anything else you wish to share...

FINAL NOTES....

FINAL NOTES....

FINAL NOTES....

USE THE FOLLOWING PAGES FOR CERTIFICATES, AWARDS. PHOTO'S ETC..

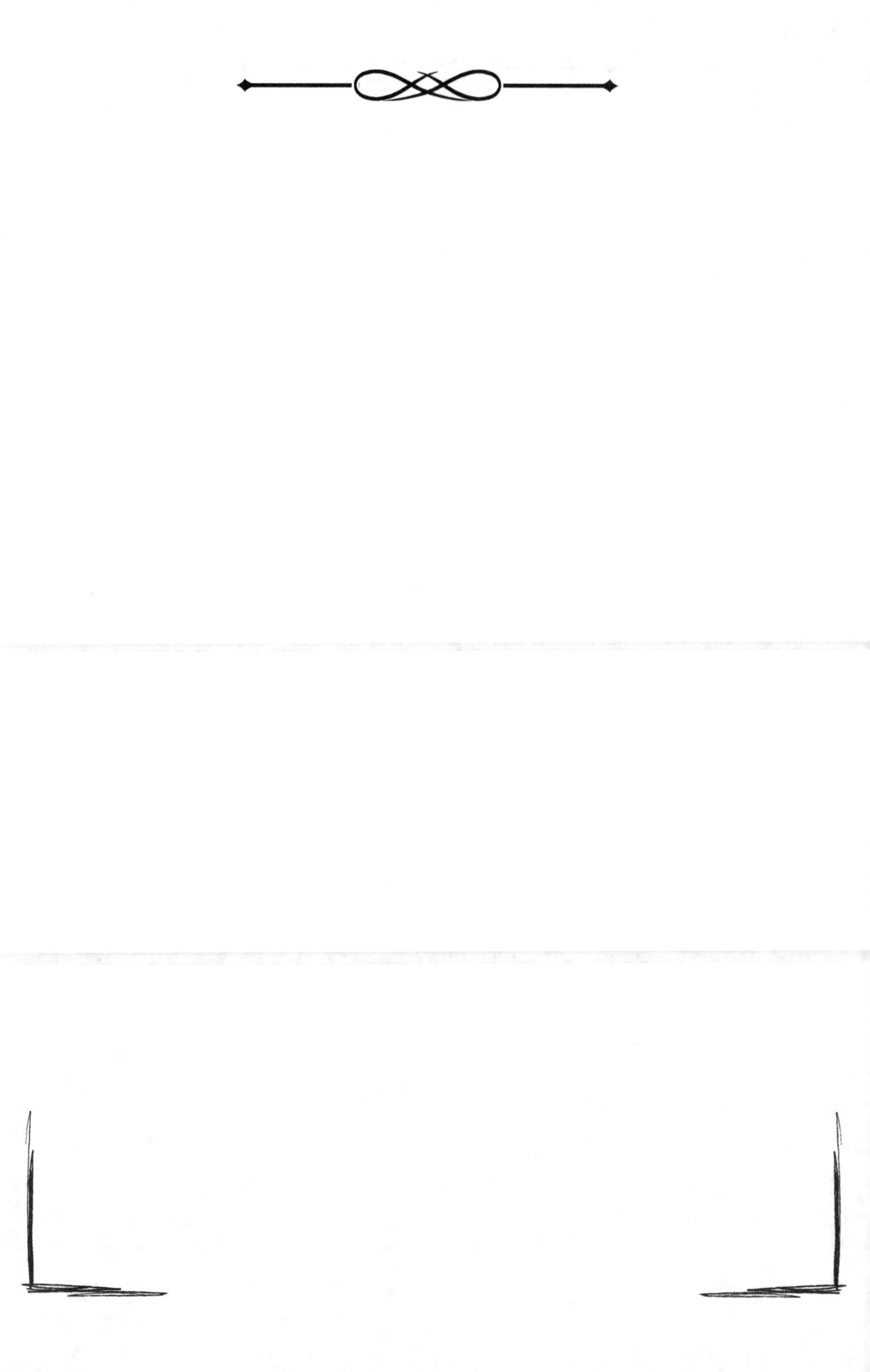

THANK YOU FOR SHARING YOUR LIFE STORY

This book was created by

Romney Nelson

OTHER BOOKS
BY
The Life Graduate Publishing Group